The Angel's Addendum

The Angel's Addendum

SAMUEL FAULK
JILLIAN CALAHAN

ANDEAN PUBLISHING
NEW YORK, NY

Copyright © 2024 by Samuel Faulk

All rights reserved. No part of this publication may be reproduced, distributed or transmitted in any form or by any means, including photocopying, recording, or other electronic or mechanical methods, without the prior written permission of the publisher, except in the case of brief quotations embodied in critical reviews and certain other noncommercial uses permitted by copyright law. For permission requests, write to the publisher, addressed "Attention: Permissions Coordinator," at the address below.

Andean Publishing
1420 York Avenue
New York, NY 10021
www.andeanpublishing.com

Publisher's Note: This is a work of fiction. Names, characters, places, and incidents are a product of the author's imagination. Locales and public names are sometimes used for atmospheric purposes. Any resemblance to actual people, living or dead, or to businesses, companies, events, institutions, or locales is completely coincidental.

Book Layout by Jeremy Taylor; www.instagram.com/jeremy.taylor.ny

Library of Congress Control Number: 2022915735
The Angel's Addendum/ Samuel Faulk/ Jillian Calahan.—1st ed.

ISBN: 978-1-7361277-5-9 (paperback)

The Angel's Addendum, **Second Book in**

The Celestial Compendium

"There are no secrets better kept
than the secrets that everybody guesses."

—George Bernard Shaw, Mrs. Warren's Profession (1893), Act III

The Angel's Addendum

A

Abandon, v. and n.

The wheels of my car[1]
spun out in the driveway.

I watched you through the
rearview mirror.

You called my name
but I couldn't hear you
through the echo of my anger.

I never thought it would be
the last time I ever saw you.

S.F.

---

[1] *The Devil's Thesaurus pg. 2*

Restraint, n.

I agonized for weeks
about whether or not
to tell you.

My smile concealing
the heartbreaking truth
hidden behind my teeth.

After all,
I had stopped.
You didn't need to know.

The magnets that
pulled me away
reversed their polarity.

S.F.

Abnormal, adj.

Things were never
the same between us
after that.

It was as if,
in losing myself,
I had forgotten who you were.

Your contours blurred
in an undefined void,
fading into obscurity.

S.F.

Customary, *adj.*

I started the tradition
of leaving each other little notes
scattered around the house
shortly after I moved in.

The notes were fragments
of a connection cocooned
in stardust.

I wanted you to know
that I was always thinking of you,
even if I wasn't around.

S.F.

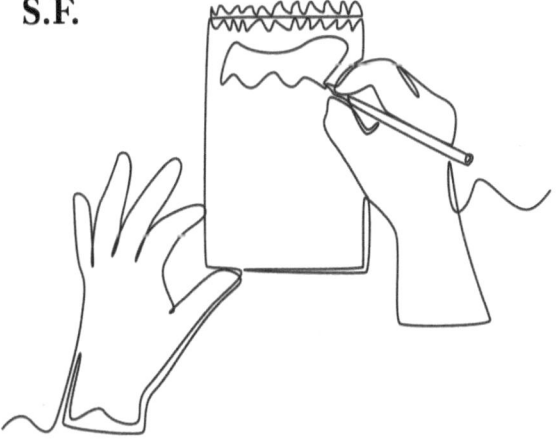

Adopt, v.

The little guinea pig
was my first sign that we would
make it the distance.

His squeals sometimes
a little deafening, but he was OURS.
Loud, stinky, little Piggers[2]
made us a family.

S.F.

---
[2] *The Devil's Thesaurus pg. 8*

Neglect, v.

I knew something was wrong
the day you left
beard hairs in the sink.
You knew I hated it.

What does it say when we stop
caring for the little things
in each other's lives?

S.F.

B

Banish, v.

When you were angry
you used to slam the bedroom door,
leaving me on the other side,
exiled from your world,
and begging to be let back in.

S.F.

Allow, v.

I didn't give *him* a key.
I unlocked the door
and beckoned from inside.

I gave *him* a tour of my soul,
opening doors and
turning on lights that hadn't
been used in years.

The only doors I kept locked
were the ones you hid behind.

S.F.

Barter, n. and v.

There were days
I bargained with God.
I prayed you would die
rather than learn the truth.

S.F.

***Possess,* v.**

I guess I went with *him*
to prove to myself that
you didn't own me.

A rebellion against the
chains of ~~marriage~~ ownership
constricting
my neck, slowly cutting off
air.

S.F.

Bereft, adj.

Every day I thought
about telling you
filled my belly with dread.

S.F.

Happy, adj.

I did not know
a single person
could mean so
much to me
until you came along.

S.F.

C

Carnal, adj.

With *him*, my body moved
but my soul stayed.
All I could think of was you
and the crimson scarf.

S.F.

Spiritual, adj.

I always knew that you
had placed me on a throne.

I drank in your praise[3]
like I was dying of thirst.

That was, until
the wine soured.

Leaving me utterly parched.

S.F.

---

3   *The Devil's Thesaurus* pg. 31

Celibate, adj. and n.

If only.
If only.
If only.
If only.
If only.
If only.
If only.

S.F.

Promiscuous, adj.

Some nights, it wasn't even about *him*.
I just needed to escape
my own thoughts.

He seemed as good
a place as any
to run to.

S.F.

Cheat, n. and v.

One night, as *he* laid next to me,
I looked over and saw a photo
of *him* and *her*.

I realized in that moment,
we were all
hurting someone we loved.

S.F.

Honest, adj.

You knew everything about me
from my hair
down to the ink on
my ankle tattoo.

You knew everything.
How could you still love me?

S.F.

Desire, n. and v.

There is so much more
than crimson scarves
and dancing hips.

There's the spark
in your eye as you tell
a joke I've heard 500 times.

There's the comforting pull
of your arms at night
as you soothe the nightmares
before they come.

S.F.

Antipathy, n.

Every morning I would stand
in front of the mirror
hoping to see a change.

What I saw only cemented my fear
as I touched the growing
speed bump on my belly.

S.F.

Doctrine, n.

I drank in your praise,
intoxicated by every word and phrase,
until the wine soured.

How could I tell you
I didn't need to be worshiped?
I needed to be loved.

S.F.

Skeptic, n.

The doubts started creeping in.
I suspected you were
doing the same thing I was.

I found no lipstick on your collar,
nor phone number in your jeans,
nor scent of betrayal or regret.

Maybe I just couldn't trust you
since I could no longer trust
myself.

S.F. & J.C.

Durable, adj.

Your arms around me
were the only shield
I ever needed.

Even when I was
the one you were fighting,
it always surprised me
when you laid
your armor at my feet.

S.F.

Fragile, *adj.*

I gave you my heart.
I plucked the glass orb from
between my ribs
even as I started to bleed.

I offered it with no expectation
of changing our lives.
How wrong I was.

S.F.

E

Eccentric, adj. and n.

I dyed my hair
and covered my skin with ink
so that when you called me beautiful,
maybe I'd believe it, too.

S.F.

Normal, *adj. and n.*

You smiled when you saw spines where heels should be.
Overflowing bookshelves[4] in place of flats.

I know I wasn't what you expected at first.
It's like you almost wanted to argue about shoes.

But books were my accessory.
I never left home without one.

No one else accepted my dance with Homer
like you did. Or quoted Plath along with me.

The way we could talk about poets and princes
made everything else seem mundane.

S.F. & J.C.

---

[4] *The Devil's Thesaurus pg. 83*

Ensnare, v.

You were late, even though you begged
me to come to your party.

I leaned against the wall,
letting the music wash over me.

He winked at me from
across the room.

A silent, alluring
invitation.

Unable to find you, I
ambled towards my fate.

S.F.

***Release*, v. and n.**

I prayed that you would die
so that I didn't feel
trapped anymore.

I prayed that you would die
so that I wouldn't
be sinning anymore.

I prayed that you would die
so that I could move
the hell on.

S.F.

Eulogy, n.

I've always wondered
what it would be like
at my funeral.
I hope I'm still your angel,
even with clipped wings.

S.F. & J.C.

Slander, n. and v.

The worst thing I could ever
say about you is that
you cared too much.

I wished you never had.
I wished you would scream
all the truths I know of myself.

I wished you would hate me.
It would be so much easier
if you were angry.

S.F.

F

Fable, n.

Helen of Troy's beauty
launched a thousand ships to war.

Rex ran from fate until he
ended up blinded by his own hand.

Vanity and pride
make us do terrible things.

S.F.

Reality, n.

Truth turned my gut
as I stared at those
two pink lines.

Was it yours or
was it *his*?

S.F.

Fervor, n.

Is the headache of tomorrow
worth tricking time for just one night
and trying to forget
the fire of *his* skin on mine?

I'm hoping this amber liquid
scorches the wrinkles of my brain
so that my neurons stop firing
when I hear *his* name.

S.F.

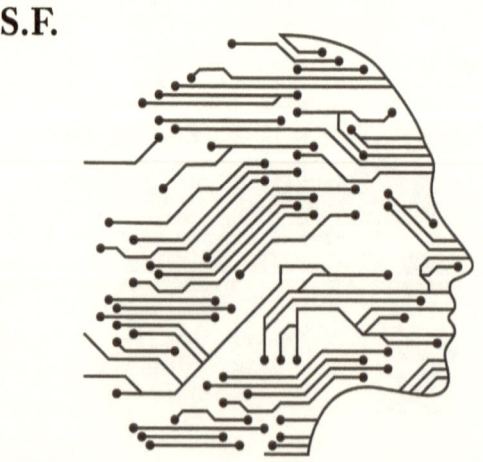

***Apathy*, n.**

After awhile I almost stopped trying to hide it.

I started putting on makeup[5] before going to see *him*.

At least *he* called me beautiful.

S.F.

---

5   The Devil's Thesaurus pg. 33

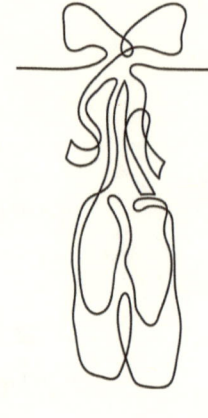

Finesse, n. and v.

Ballet was the only way to
drown out the noise
in my head.

Spinning, bouncing, jumping.
If I kept moving, I couldn't hear
my own thoughts.

As soon as I stopped moving,
the thoughts would tumble,
like a failed tour jeté.

S.F.

Ignorance, n.

I realized too late
how much you loved me.
I'm sorry I didn't know.
I'm sorry I didn't see it.
I'm sorry.

S.F.

Genuine, adj.

For your birthday I surprised you
with a typewriter[6]. You were always writing,
and I wanted to be a part of that world.

You spent so long in your office
typing away, it was easy to
slip out of the front door unnoticed.

S.F.

---

6   The Devil's Thesaurus pg. 98

Dishonest, adj.

Soon, every word I said
was shrouded in smoke
and misdirection.

In the knotted interlacing of
my own creations,
it became difficult to
keep the stories straight.
I forgot my own lies.

Call me the amnesiac architect.

S.F.

Guilt, n. and v.

You moved money around
as if I wouldn't notice our savings
dwindling like the chips
in your poker game.

S.F.

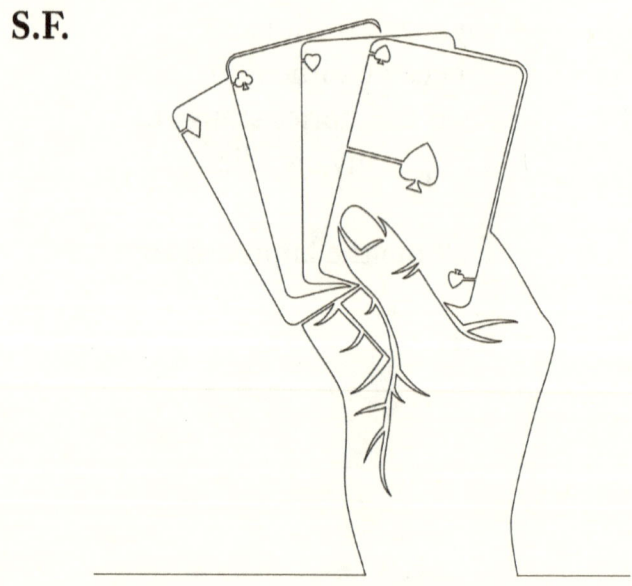

Innocence, n.

I wore white to remind myself,
of who I was and who I would be.

I wore white to feel redeemed,
and, for a moment, I felt free.

I wore white to erase the stains
of my past mistakes.

I wore white to remind myself
that I am more than heartache.

S.F.

Gluttony, n.

Is it so bad I craved more?
More praise spoken with kisses.
More head-spinning attention.

More whispered words of affection
stolen under a starless night sky.
More excitement, like lightning in my veins.

More of anything I asked for.
It all seemed so endless;
a bottomless appetite.
He offered me the limitless
feast I craved.

S.F.

***Satisfaction*, n.**

When I passed my first exam we were so excited that we popped open a bottle of wine I was saving for *him*.

S.F.

H

Habitual, adj.

The days of the week were blurred together.
Distinguished by only what to eat and watch.
Mondays were my green salad and murder mysteries.
Tuesdays were your chicken and comedies.
Wednesdays were my tacos and action movies.

Thursdays were your chicken alfredo and romcoms.
Fridays were our leftovers and reruns.
Saturdays were coffee in our pjs with fried eggs.
We watched each other.
Sundays were chicken salad after church.
I hate your chicken[7].

S.F.

---

7   The Devil's Thesaurus pg. 280

Spontaneous, adj.

As you left for work, I yelled *Wait!*
and chased after you.

Your hand on the door,
I spun you around and kissed you
for the first time in months.
The spark rekindled for a moment.

S.F.

Heartfelt, adj.

You plucked words
from between your ribs,
one by one,
as you wrote poetry
on my skin.

But I just kept
washing them away.

J.C.

False, adj.

Until death do us part.
The only promise
I ever kept.

J.C.

Heathen, adj. and n.

Do we blame the woman bathing
on the roof[8], or the man who
claimed her and sent her husband to die?
Is the sin of submission all that bad?

S.F.

---

8   2 Samuel 11:2-6, 14-15 (NIV)

Sacred, adj.

We built an altar of whispered words,
lit candles of broken promises
and chanted our creed
of what it meant to love.

A devotion of desperation,
as if praying would
mend our brokenness.

S.F.

I

Illuminate, v.

For so long
you were the light
at my feet.

I've always
feared
the dark.

S.F.

Obscure, adj and v.

One throwaway
comment made while
watching television,
but you remembered what I said.
I can't believe you bought
the pearl necklace I'd always wanted.

S.F.

Immanent, adj.

The concept of motherhood
always scared me. What if I can't
nurture as nature intended?

What if I can't love
anyone more than I loved you?

S.F.

Extrinsic, adj.

I can feel your love[9] covering
my skin like a blanket or
the ink of my tattoos.

Your love clings to me like
Orange Blossom Body Lotion.
Why can't I wash it away?

S.F.

---
9   Hamlet: 2.2.115-118

Indulge, v.

Your kisses were smooth dark chocolate soothing emotions I didn't know I had.

His were hard cinnamon jawbreakers dancing on my tongue until I couldn't speak.

You never even noticed the silence.

S.F.

Stifle, *v.*

It's 3 a.m., and I'm sneaking back into bed
beside you, hoping not to wake you.

In the corner of the room,
Piggers squeaks for the mother
he never gets to see.

S.F.

Jeer, n. and v.

We were soft once.
Until our fights quaked
the very foundation
of the home we built together.

The aftershocks
became more prevalent,
and we vowed to never
become like our parents.

But sometimes I hear
my father in your voice
and I can't help
but shudder.

J.C.

Commend, v.

As my belly grew,
I didn't feel worthy of
a stranger's attention.

Everyone said *Congratulations!*;
that hollow and empty word.
As if this was what I wanted.

S.F.

Jejune, adj.

Thank you for tolerating it
for so long. I know it's silly,
but Disney movies[10] are the only
things that help me sleep.

Nothing says *escape from reality*
like a good ol' fairy tale.

S.F.

---

10   The Devil's Thesaurus pg. 112

Elegance, n.

Our wedding day was the
most beautiful I ever felt.
The mermaid silhouette
flared into fantasy where
I could feel like a part of the ocean.

But the layers of silk and lace
concealed reality,
while the veil
hid my fractured smile.

S.F.

Jilted, adj.

I had my bags packed for weeks.
Ready to fly towards freedom.
My wings flexed and unfurled
every time we fought.

That Night
as you screamed,
I grabbed my bag
and flew from our nest.

S.F.

Cherished, adj.

You carried a picture of me,
bent and worn,
inside your wallet.

I was always safe
in your pocket.
Will you still keep me there?

J.C.

K

Kerfuffle, n.

I still don't understand
why you went to bed
right after dinner. Leaving me
to clean up in your wake.

S.F.

Tranquility, n.

And, all at once,
there was a bright light
heading towards me.
The anger, the pain,
all meant nothing,
as my entire world
suddenly burst into calm.

J.C.

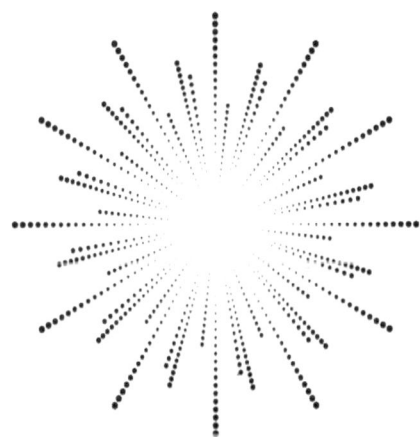

Kithe, v.

I wrote you a poem[11] today.
It's our six-month anniversary
and I wanted to show you I could write too.

But how could I ever measure up
to the eloquence of a college English professor?
I'll keep it safe in this drawer
until I'm ready.

S.F.

---

11   The Devil's Thesaurus pg. 186

Repudiate, v.

I sat there praying for one
pink line. Bile rose in my throat
when I saw two.

Porcelain turned into cement;
linoleum into a prison cell;
and my body was the prisoner,
charged with deceiving
me so terribly.

S.F.

Knowingly, adj.

Somehow, it made it worse
that *he* knew about you.

That our marriage was no longer the secret
tucked beneath my breast.

After all, I never understood how *he*
could shake your hand at work.

S.F.

Inept, adj.

I was so scared of
becoming like my mother
I didn't notice when I had
become like my father.
A man fond of clandestine trysts.
Apparently, midnight meetings
ran in the family.

S.F.

L

Lacerate, v.

Tonight, the flashbacks
cut right to the bone.
My wounds, evident.
I stitched myself back together
with your heartstrings.

J.C.

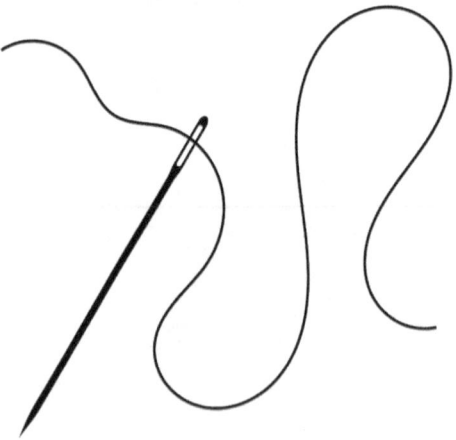

Mend, v.

I picked up the pieces
of our lives and your
grandfather's pocket watch.
Maybe if I could fix it,
time would rewind
and I could stop myself from
throwing it to the ground
in the first place.

S.F.

Livid, adj.

I wonder if our neighbors
heard you scream
when I said *his* name
instead of yours.

With such guttural rage,
I don't know how
the walls around us
stayed standing.

J.C.

Sanguine, *adj.*

You whispered
I love you,
feather soft and hopeful.
I didn't answer
as I nuzzled further
into your neck.

J.C.

Lover, n.

How can I compare an inferno
to a candle in the dead of night?
You give light and warmth.
He scorches the leaves from the forest.
Neither will last forever.

S.F.

***Carper*, n.**

I knew I made a mistake
when I told *him* about
the growing bump in my belly
and *he* smirked, then made a joke
about a coat hanger. Something
you never would have said.

S.F.

m

Magical, adj.

You spun tales of
knights rescuing princesses
in such a way I believed you.

I believed you when you said
the light I held in my fingertips[12]
was your only warmth.

I believed you when you said
you would move mountains
to bring a smile to my face.

I believed you when you said
that we would last forever.
I believed you.

S.F.

---

12   The Devil's Thesaurus pg. 102

Ordinary, adj.

Soon, every word I said
was shrouded in smoke
and misdirection.

Lies became my first language.
Pouring from my mouth
as smooth as wine.

Deception became so much
of who I was that I didn't recognize
the face in the mirror.

S.F.

Merry, adj.

Our favorite holiday was Christmas.
We'd spend an entire weekend
hanging lights and decorating the tree.

We even got Piggers his own tiny stocking.

You always smirked as you hung the mistletoe
in the doorframe of our bedroom.

But this year, I let it gather dust
in the corner of the attic.
You never asked where it was.

J.C.

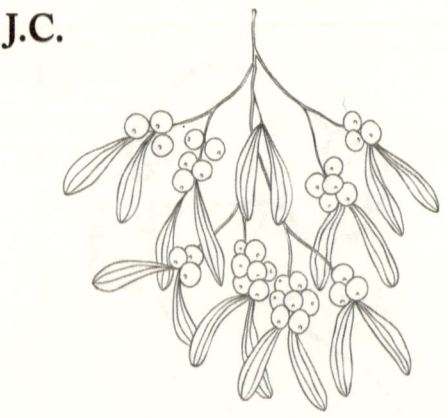

Despondent, adj.

I almost told you
the day after it happened.

While I still had
the scent of *him* clinging to my skin.

I almost told you as soon
as I woke up next to you.

Even though I was thinking
about *him* and the void you couldn't fill.

I almost told you
but I lost courage when *he* called.

S.F.

Move, v.

You memorized the way
my body moved in the dark.

Could magnetize my hips to yours
because you knew just how
to hold onto a shadow.

You knew every place to kiss
that wouldn't spark the trauma
hidden beneath my skin.
Not even *he* knew
how to do that.

J.C.

Stay, v.

The last few months, we fell asleep,
backs against the cold chasm between us.
I love you could echo through that space
if either of us would just say it.
But we didn't.

When we woke up face-to-face,
it was the first time in a long time
that I stared into your eyes.

They were etched with pain
and I held the chisel.
Your voice shook
as it trembled over the words:
Please stay.

J.C.

Narrow, adj.

The divide
between my
head and
my heart
is as
vast as
the abyss
in my
father's gaze
struggling to
recognize me.

I felt
so small
admitting the
truth to
him, I
could fold
myself into
an apology.
He won't
remember anyway.

S.F.

***Spacious**, adj.*

I've lost count of the stars.
There's just too much space
in between us.

J.C.

Night, n.

There are times when I wish the starless twilight would smother me in a blanket of my own sins and swaddle me in a cocoon of memories[13], be them sins, or pleasure, or both.

S.F.

---

13 The Odyssey *Book XX, Lines 56-58*

Day, n. [14]

Sunlight peeked through curtains
to signal a new morning.
I opened my eyes to you inching towards me.

I rolled out of bed, away from morning breath
wondering how I got so lucky
to be with a man worth waking up next to.

S.F.

---

14   The Devil's Thesaurus pg. 165

Noisy, adj.

Click. Click.
I turn up the sound
of the T.V. as it flashes
through the darkness,
lighting up the walls
of our bedroom.

The fan, set to high,
oscillates in the corner.
And the sounds of 3 a.m.
float through the open window.
Cars passing by.
Crickets chirping.
An owl that's never known
what it feels like
to be torn in two.

Click. Click. Click.
I turn the volume up more.
Anything to muffle
the hum of my sorrow.
To cover the sound
of you breathing next to me.

J.C.

Silent*, *adj.

After you slammed the door,
the house grew quiet.
So quiet I could hear
my heartbeat bounce
from room to room,
as though it were searching
for another's chest
to bury itself in.

And I contemplated
setting fire to our bed
just to hear the alarms.
To hear anything but the sound
of my heart breaking.

J.C.

Obedient, adj.

Another headache.
You bring me water
and tell me to drink.

I roll my eyes as I take a sip
and leave the glass full
on the counter.

Yet I would swallow oceans for *him*.
I would drown for *him*.
And maybe that's why
I can never seem
to catch my breath.

J.C.

Recalcitrant, adj.

You used to laugh at my stubbornness.
The way I would fall asleep on the couch
and insist I wasn't tired when
you'd gently wake me to go to bed.

Or when I would get so frustrated
you could see my left eye twitch
and you would kiss it to make it stop.

You used to laugh at my stubbornness.
Until I refused to breathe,
even for God.

J.C.

Obvious, adj.

Everything happened
in the shadows of *his* bedroom.
Sequestered beneath the sheets
and hidden behind closed blinds.

Until the day *he* reached for my hand.
The same day I kissed *him* under the sun.
Everything we kept in the dark
came to a blazing light,
so bright it blinded you
from the truth.

J.C.

Ambiguous, adj.

My heart sank
down,
    down,
        down,
plunging deep into
my trembling gut,
as your words echoed
through the heavy air:

We need to talk.

J.C.

Offer, v.

I remember, in the beginning,
holding my heart out to you
in the form of an open diary.

If you knew my thoughts,
maybe you'd understand me better.
Or at least know why I write.

S.F.

***Revoke*, v.**

We are nothing more
than remnants of
an abandoned house.
Full of dust and
shattered memories.

Where love is a squatter,
lingering in an empty living room,
just waiting for us to come home.
But would it even recognize us
if we knocked?

J.C.

Permanent, adj.

You read me the poems you wrote
long before we ever met,
about a woman just like me.

She had my smile.
It curved in the rounded letters
you so deftly wrote upon the page.
I could almost hear my laugh
between the lines.

You acted as though our love
sprang from your pen.
And as long as those words
remained on the page,
we would be okay.

But not all ink stains.
What's deemed permanent
can be erased.
It just takes a little alcohol
and a mischievous smile
to smear everything
you never thought would fade.

J.C.

Temporary, adj.

One glance.
One smile.
One hello.

One drink.
One dance.
One embrace.

One kiss.
One decision.
One night.

He was supposed to be
my one regret.
Not you.

J.C.

Persevere, v.

I swallow it down,
the burning bile of unsaid words
held hostage in my throat.

One day at a time,
I climb to the peak of my regret
and call my bluff.

You're not even here to see it.
Now the only way out,
is back down.

S.F. & J.C.

Falter, v.

A budding flower
on the edge of bloom
grows in my gullet.
Its thorns, sharp
and whetted,
catch on the walls
of my throat.

It hurts holding this in
because I know it will break you.
It's like having to choose
which one of us to cut.
When in the end
both of us will bleed.

J.C.

Prudent, adj.

I kept my clothes on at home[15],
not because I was shy
but because I couldn't imagine
being so vulnerable with
another person.

To lie bare without pretense
or assumptions was something
I had never experienced outside of you.

I kept waiting for hungry eyes
to morph into selfish hands,
but all you could do was give.

S.F. & J.C.

---

15 The Devil's Thesaurus pg. 190

Reckless, adj.

You grabbed my hips
and we danced in the kitchen,
like old times.

Ellington. Coltrane. Holiday.
All floating through smoke,
cutting through our bitterness.

We let dinner burn,
as though the music
were the only thing
keeping us alive.

J.C.

Q

Quality, n.

I looked down at
your grandmother's wedding ring.
The diamonds alone could pay
for our house. (Or my new life.)

You were screaming at me
about *him* again.
Tears streamed down my face.
It was time to leave.

The beating carbon in my chest
cracked and embers fell in anger.
I threw the ring, but it bounced
off your arm and rolled back to my feet...

S.F. & J.C.

Inferiority, n.

Of course, I knew
what our friends said
behind our backs.
I heard the whispers.

The cold shoulder
turned into a sheet
of ice thick enough
to walk over.

S.F.

Quell, v.

I swallow it down,
the burning bile
in my throat.

6 months from now
it will all have
been worth it.

Or will it?

J.C.

Amplify, v.

The words started as a whisper
in the back of my mind.

Words I wasn't ready to say.
I don't love you anymore.

As soon as they fell from my lips
these words grew and raged like an inferno,

burning down everything we had built,
leaving the taste of ash in my mouth.

S.F.

Question, n.

A sideways glance.
A devilish grin.
He took my hand
and I gladly followed.
He didn't even have to ask.

J.C.

Answer, n. and v.

He didn't have to ask
and I didn't have to respond
with my voice; my hips said
what my lips dared not speak.

Our silent dialogue left
no room for ambiguity or
hesitance.

S.F.

や

Rare, adj.

You glanced lovingly at me
over your marbled cobalt steak.
I hadn't seen that spark in your eyes
in so long, I nearly forgot what
it looked like to be appreciated.

S.F. & J.C.

Quotidian, adj.

I plucked the smudged cup[16]
from your hands
and sighed.

Is this what marriage is?
Fixing your mistakes
for the rest of our lives?

S.F.

---
16   The Devil's Thesaurus pg. 143

Romantic, adj.

I laid out rose petals
from the front door
to the bedroom
and grabbed the crimson scarf
before slipping under the covers.

I never paid attention
to things like three-month anniversaries,
but maybe you were changing my mind
and it was making me sentimental.

As I quivered with anticipation,
my excited grin turned sour.
While I waited for *him*
all I could think of was you.

S.F.

Practical, adj.

I was always the pragmatist
having to pull on your heartstrings.
Like bringing a kite back from the sky.

How often did I wish to cut myself free from
my concrete shoes that held me to the ground
and look for
you
        among
                the
                      clouds.

S.F.

Rigid, adj.

How many nights
have I slept
curled at the edges
of myself
and the bed?
Unable to unfurl
because it meant
having to face
what I had done.

J.C.

Flexible, adj.

Turns out,
it was easy
to bend
to *his* will.
Turns out,
I'm nothing
but spineless.
A blade of grass,
bowing to
the slightest touch.

J.C.

S

Serious, adj.

When I unpacked the toilet paper
for the first time and put it in place,
your nostrils flared.

You laughed with a smile
that did not meet your eyes.

S.F.

Trivial, adj.

Your eyes lit up when I
complimented your new tie.

I smiled and said it looked great.
You wore *his* favorite color well.

S.F.

Strenuous, adj.

I started ballet again as a way to
recapture the joy of my youth
and somehow still feel
like a swan in flight.

Every leap, every pirouette,
a reminder of the strenuous effort
needed to maintain this facade of grace.

Are my muscles strained,
or is it my patience?

S.F.

Feeble, adj.

My dad's mind started going before I knew it. Is anyone ever ready for their father to forget them?

S.F.

Scatterbrained, adj.

I was so angry when I drove
away from you.
Tears streamed down my face.
These pages sat beside me,
already stained with water and regret.

The cover of a starless night
was perfect to hide
these words from you.
My attempt at rewriting myself.

As my words slid along the page,
rain slicked the road,
making me skid further
away from you.

I didn't see the truck
until it was too late.

S.F. & J.C.

Shrewd, adj.

He smiled, shook your hand,
and introduced *himself.*

Started at the university[17] a few
weeks ago and liked it well enough.

When *he* smiled at me with a different smile,
a cold fire spread through my chest.

S.F.

---

17   See Knowingly pg. 86

Taboo, adj., n., and v.

The phone light blinked
in the dead of night.
A beacon of everything
I couldn't resist.

You never questioned
the slight arch of my lips,
curled in a 3 a.m. smile.
You never questioned
how my eyes lit up
brighter than the screen.

And you never questioned
why I started sleeping with
my phone under my pillow.

When I told you it was my cousin,
one you had never met,
you didn't ask anything more.

So, of course, I didn't tell.
I think we both knew
what it really meant.

S.F. & J.C.

Encourage, v.

Quietly, I bring you milk and cookies
and kiss the top of your head
as you sit at the typewriter,
composing your latest book of poetry.

Silently, I back away,
reassuring you it's okay
to skip our favorite shows
for the third time this week.

Without a sound, I slip out the front door.
You're engulfed in words and ink,
and will never even know
I left to be with *him*.

J.C.

Thirst, n.

His lips tasted of spiced mead,
warming all the frigid places
I kept hidden in the darkness.
I was buzzing with love.

One that ~~wouldn't~~ couldn't last,
and you thought me waspish.[18]
But how many times did I sting you?
How many times did you let me?

J.C.

---

18   *The Taming Of The Shrew 2.1.222-223*

Fertile, adj.

I started pushing you away
when your fingers
danced across my skin,
hoping to bloom a giggle
from beneath my roots.

But there was just too much mud,
too much silt and muck for me
to pull joy up through dirt
and plant it on my face.

I had no capacity to
dig that deep.

I stopped smiling.
I stopped laughing
at your jokes
when we became one.

J.C.

Timorous, adj.

I talked a lot about
my favorite English professor.
Until you asked to meet *him*.

S.F.

Forthcoming, adj.

Filling out paperwork
to protect the growing bump
in my belly
just seemed like
the right thing to do.

The drumbeat of life
and the ocean's roar
filled my ears as I stared
at the line that read
Life Insurance Beneficiary.
(Do I put *his* name or yours?)

S.F.

u

Unconscious, adj.

Just a few sips
of red wine.

I never got a chance
to say *no*.

J.C.

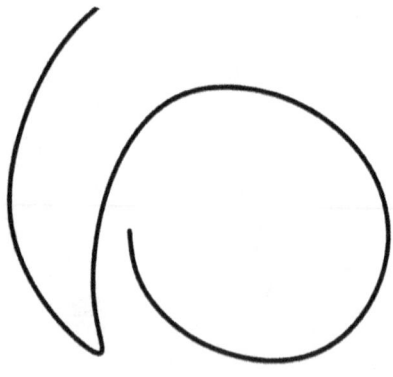

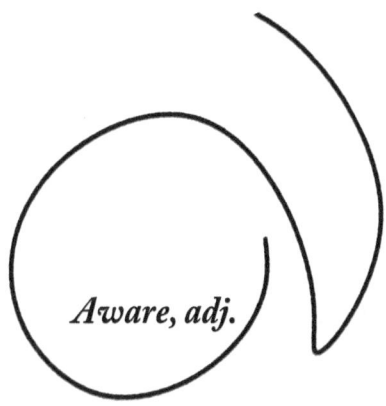

Aware, adj.

I knew exactly what I was doing
when I turned and winked.

I lured *him* into a citrine sunset
dusting the lids of my emerald eyes.

He lost *his* way down an agate path
and found refuge in my ruby-painted lips.

All while we forged a love
made from zirconia and fool's gold.

My worth felt tawdry at best.
I just wanted to be good enough
…for someone.

J.C.

Unknown, adj. and n.

You never got the chance
to be called Dad.
Even if we had survived,
the title could have been his.
We'll never know.

J.C.

***Proverbial,* adj.**

They say insanity
is repeating the same thing
over and over again,
expecting different results:

I love you.
I love you.
I love you.
I love you.

J.C.

Upset, v., n., and adj..

It's the little things, you know.

Taking out the garbage.
Setting the table.
Kissing me goodnight.

You forgot.
You forgot.
You forgot.

J.C.

***Stabilize**, v.*

At some point, we fractured.
    and what hurt worse
        than the break
was realigning the pieces.

J.C.

Vacant, adj.

You used to tell me
how I stole your heart
and took your breath away.
I know you meant figuratively,
but it seems I'm
more literal than I thought.
Oh, how I've left you
so empty.

J.C.

Overflowing, adj. and v.

We were two rivers
   flowing towards the sea.
      Steady, stable, safe.
         Until we reached a confluence.
         An amalgamation of bodies,
      hearts and souls thought to be
     unbreakable through any storm,
   come hell or high water.
We watched the current rise.
The rush and the rapids,
   had nothing on us.
      We managed to survive but
         somewhere along the meandering
        a tributary appeared.
          A river can only take so much
       before it breaches its banks.
     Never once did I think
   of the collateral damage
from a flood of my own making.
  Never once did I think
I'd just watch as you drowned.

J.C.

Vacillate, v.

I prayed for guidance
along Eden's path,
searching for answers
within lush greenery.

But I found nothing in the garden.
Nothing between petals
or beneath the leaves.

Until a single apple fell at my feet.
A morsel of destiny,
dripping with the nectar of choice.

It was the sweetest bite
I had ever tasted.

J.C.

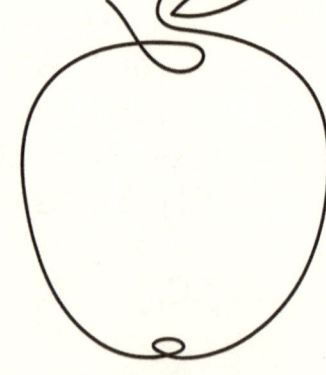

Resolute, adj.

You looked me in the eye
trying to convince me
your dad's broken fishing rod
was worth keeping.

The reel was broken,
and the line was cut short.
What did you expect to catch
besides a boat full of empty promises?

S.F.

Voluntary, adj. and n.

As I opened the cupboard
to retrieve my favorite snack,
a slip of paper fluttered to the ground.
A note you must have written long ago,
because it read
"I'll love you until the end of time."

I never asked you to write these reminders,
but they are seared in my mind all the same.

I wonder when you noticed
I had stopped writing them.
I wonder how many you'll find
once I'm gone.

S.F.

Compulsory, adj.

You washed the crimson scarf
with the whites and didn't understand
why I was upset as
I held a rose reminder
of your forgetfulness.

Yes. Of course, we have to wash them separately. I hiss;
years of venom in my voice.

Stains last forever.

S.F. & J.C.

W

Wealth, n.

My lips are heavy
with the weight of secrets,
but I continue to bite my tongue.
I never knew lies
taste like pennies.

J.C.

***Poverty,* n.**

How many times
did I shatter my knees,
pleading with you to stay?
My palms open in supplication.
I shouldn't have to beg
to be loved.

J.C.

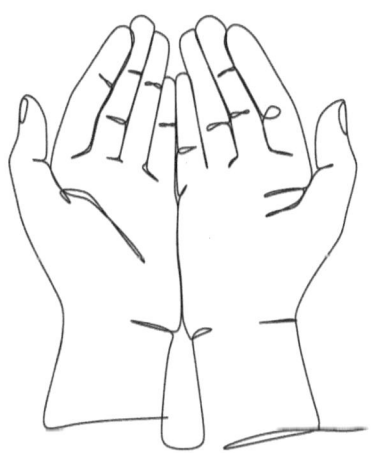

Wild, adj. and n.

For weeks, I had forgotten
to water the garden.
You used to say that I
had a gangrene thumb.
With a little love,
the flowers will come back,
but I won't.
I've become a wasteland.
There's no coming back from this.

J.C.

Tame, adj. and v.

I miss wildness.
Taking something abandoned
and making it beautiful.
All feral blossoms and savage overgrowth.

I miss the blue thrill of waves
against my chest.
I miss the lioness.

And, oh, how I miss the burning.
The rapaciousness of flames.
This wild vanished in the
softness of your hands.

Melted into your body until I
no longer knew where your civilized
tongue started and my wild ended.
Because it did end for a time.

But the overgrowth, the ocean, the lioness,
the flame all came back to me.
What a shame I had to
find them in *his* bed.

J.C.

Wise, adj., n., and v.

Hughes. Whitman. Plath.
The Bard. Homer. Yeats.
I am surrounded by wordsmiths

and two English professors who can't
read between the lines I crossed.

S.F. & J.C.

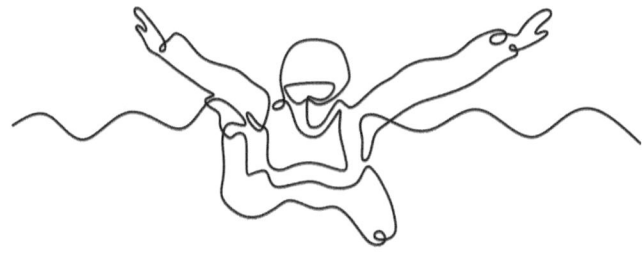

Foolish, adj.

We went skydiving together.
The first time, but not the last,
I would place my life
in your hands. I was terrified
until you held me close
and whispered one of your new poems
in my ear. I closed my eyes,
and leapt into the unknown,
    praying
        that
              you
          would
    catch
me.

S.F.

Xeric, adj.

We watched deserts form
as everything crumbled around us,
making paradise out of nothing.
When did our oasis
turn into a mirage?

J.C.

Moist, adj.

I left lipstick stains
on *his* collar.
He left fingerprints
on my heart.

J.C.

Xenial, adj.

I made a home
of his heart.
He made a hotel
of my body.

I welcomed him in.
He held no reservations.

Neither of us
found the love
we needed.

J.C.

Surly, adj.

Looking inward
I don't recognize this hate.
This wild animosity.
This self-destruction.

I miss when anger
wasn't caged behind my teeth.
When resentment wasn't all
that spilled from my mouth.

I miss when my skin
wasn't made of fire,
and when you weren't afraid
to touch me.

Somewhere along the way
I lost myself
And now you
have lost me, too.

J.C.

Xiphoid, adj.

Our
love
hardened
over time like
the center of your
ribcage. Memories
calcified into the core
of who we were, with pain
and love all forming
the curve of the
sword. Be
careful.
Love is
sharp.

S.F.

***Gaunt*, adj.**

Your patience
was as thin
as the
ice in
your
voice
when I
asked what's
for dinner
tonight.
*Fend for
yourself
like I
always do.*

S.F.

Yearning, n.

I miss when my skin
wasn't made of fire,
and when you weren't afraid
to touch me.

How I long to touch you again.
Someone else kindled the flames[19]
but you are the only one who
could tame the inferno.

S.F.

---

19   *Jane Eyre*

Negligent, adj.

On our anniversary,
you waited patiently
at the table.
Our hearts raw, blue,
seared with betrayal.
I let dinner
go cold.

J.C.

Yin, adj.

How like the Earth
that I am pulled to *him*.
Yearning to warm
the darkest parts of me.

J.C.

Yang, adj.

And oh, how like the sun
he ignites a fire within.
Slow to melt,
then quick to consume.

J.C.

You, pron.

My knight in shining armor;
who fought until my final breath.

My poet, my prince.
My protector, my provider.
You awoke in me a queen
worthy of honeyed words.

If only I believed you
when I had the chance.

S.F.

Me, pron.

Meetings late into the night.
Memories left on my neck.
Memorizing *his* body, forgetting yours.
Method acting as a happy wife.

I blamed so much on you,
when all of our problems
began with me.

J.C.

z

Zealous, adj.

I contemplated coming home
to relieve this distended heart of its guilt.
But how could I resist someone
who just couldn't get enough of me?

J.C.

Aloof, adj.

Time stood still
in the space between
our fingers.
My ring felt so heavy
as I pulled my hand
from yours.

J.C.

Zeitgeist, n.

He offered me a drink.
The same champagne
from our wedding day.
It tasted like white noise
and yesterdays.

I hope you don't get
the tinge of aftertaste
on my kiss.

J.C.

Contemporary, adj. and n.

I slipped under the covers.
The scent of rose petals
reminds me of our first walk[20]
along the riverside.

A shift of light catches my eye.
A sundress hung on the back
of the bedroom door. It
wasn't my size, and in that moment
I couldn't help but wonder
where *his* wife was tonight.

S.F. & J.C.

---

20   The Devil's Thesaurus pg. 187

Zenith, n.

We stood on the cliff side[21]
watching baby seals play
down at the water's edge.
I looked you in the eyes
as you kneeled.

Popping the question
sounded more like a bang.
Ever so softly, I whispered *yes*,
hoping the wind
wouldn't catch the echo
of a promise I wasn't ready to make.

S.F. & J.C.

---

21   The Devil's Thesaurus pg. 210

Nadir, n.

The last time I saw you[22]
was through the rearview mirror.
You called my name
but I couldn't hear you
through the echo of my anger.

The truck appeared
and I couldn't see you
anymore. All I could see were
white lights and shame.

I screamed your name instead of *his*.
You couldn't hear me through
shattering glass and crunching metal.
These pages flew into my vision.
Paper and ink were all I could see.

This book is my
final attempt at rewriting myself.
And though there were some things
I could erase, I could never erase you.

S.F. & J.C.

---

22   See Abandon, pg. 2

the end

APPENDIX

7. One evening David got up from his bed and walked around on the roof of the palace. From the roof he saw a woman bathing. The woman was very beautiful, and David sent someone to find out about her. The man said, "She is Bathsheba, the daughter of Eliam and the wife of Uriah the Hittite." Then David sent messengers to get her. She came to him, and he slept with her…The woman conceived and sent word to David, saying, "I am pregnant."…So David sent this word to Joab: "Send me Uriah the Hittite." And Joab sent him to David… In the morning David wrote a letter to Joab and sent it with Uriah. In it he wrote, "Put Uriah out in front where the fighting is fiercest. Then withdraw from him so he will be struck down and die."
~*2 Samuel 11:2-6, 14-15* (NIV)

9. "Doubt thou the stars are fire,
Doubt that the sun doth move,
Doubt truth to be a liar,
But never doubt I love."
~*Hamlet*: 2.2.115-118

13. "So, surrender to sleep at last. What a misery, keeping watch through the night, wide awake—you'll soon come up from under all your troubles."
~*The Odyssey:* XX.56-58

18. PETRUCHIO: Come, come, you wasp! I' faith, you are too angry.
KATHERINE: If I be waspish, best beware my sting.
~*The Taming of the Shrew:* 2.1.222-223

17. "He seemed to devour me with his flaming glance: physically, I felt, at the moment, powerless as stubble exposed to the draught and glow of a furnace: mentally, I still possessed my soul, and with it the certainty of ultimate safety".
~Brontë, Charlotte. *Jane Eyre*, Century Co., New York, NY, 1906, p. 339

https://babel.hathitrust.org/cgi/pt?id=mdp.39015039284404&seq=365

ABOUT THE AUTHORS

SAMUEL FAULK grew up in the beautiful Pacific Northwest. He is a librarian who views the written word as fuel for the soul. In his spare time he watches way too many shows and enjoys writing fiction/poetry.

He writes in several genres spanning poetry, fiction, and creative nonfiction memoirs. Most of his nonfiction writing is rooted in personal experience dealing with the effects of growing up with cerebral palsy, as well as finding God. He hopes to give a voice to the disabled community and bridge the gap between "Pray for healing" and "I'm comfortable with how God made me".

Faulk has been published in the *The Shrub-Steppe Poetry Journal*, as well as the Yakima Herald Republic Newspaper. He was also shortlisted for the 2023 Central Avenue Poetry Prize and will appear in the upcoming 2024 anthology. His poem *Ensnare* (from his first book) was featured and planted on a flower pot in the Lake Detroit 2023 Flowerpot Poetry Walk.

He is the author of *The Devil's Thesaurus* (August 2022), a book of fictional narrative poetry, first of the duology *The Celestial Compendium*.

Find more poetry on his TikTok: @rebornfromfire
Or his website: www.samuelfaulk.com

JILLIAN CALAHAN is a poet and short story writer from the Pacific Northwest. She has 2 dogs and 3 cats. In her free time she enjoys reading, crafting, puzzles, bookstores, walks in the woods, stargazing, and taking too many pictures of pretty sunsets.

She has been published in a variety of works including:
Not Ghosts But Spirits Vol. 1&2 (Querencia Press)
Say Her Name Poetry Anthology
(Dark Thirty Poetry Publishing)
Botany of Gaia (Quillkeepers Press)
The Story Behind The Poems Vol. 1&2
(Behind The Vision)

She was also shortlisted for the Central Avenue Poetry Prize and will be published in the upcoming 2024 Anthology.

You can find her work on
Instagram @novamarie_poetry

www.ingramcontent.com/pod-product-compliance
Lightning Source LLC
Chambersburg PA
CBHW031106080526
44587CB00011B/856